Look and Find®

123

SESAME STREET

Let's Go to the ZOO!

pi kids®

publications international, ltd.

Elmo loves the zoo! The zoo is a place where animals of all different shapes and sizes live. The first animals Elmo sees are the lions and the tigers.

Can you find these signs showing where Elmo might go next?

SEA LIONS

ZEBRAS

PETTING ZOO

PENGUINS

BUTTERFLIES

MONKEYS

REPTILE HOUSE

Sing this song to the tune of "The Wheels on the Bus."

The lions at the zoo go grrr, grrr, ROAR! Animals are great!

SOUVENIRS

MONKEYS

ELEPHANTS

SEA LIONS

Elmo says good-bye to land lions and hello to sea lions! Sea lions are excellent swimmers. Elmo loves to watch them swim and play.

Search the scene for these silly sea lions and some friends:

The sea lions at the zoo go splash, splash, splash! Animals are great!

After watching the sea lions splash, Elmo heads off to the warm and dry Savanna exhibit. A savanna is land that's grassy and open.

Look around the savanna habitat for these animals:

this antelope

this giraffe

this zebra

this meerkat

this gazelle

this ostrich

this elephant

♪ *The giraffes at the zoo have long, long necks! Animals are great!* ♪

Elmo goes from the warm savanna to another heated habitat—the reptile and amphibian house. Reptiles and amphibians are cold-blooded. That means their bodies don't stay warm on their own, so they like warm environments. Some amphibians live part of their life underwater and part of their life on land!

Can you find these reptiles and amphibians?

tree snake

this red-eyed tree frog

this chameleon

this salamander

a water dragon

gecko

boa constrictor

The snakes at the zoo go slither, slither, HISS! Animals are great!

"Oooh-ooh-ahh-ahh!" Elmo thinks he's a monkey! Search around this amazing indoor jungle habitat for monkeys and other animals:

♪ The monkeys at the zoo go
Ooh! Ooh! Ooh!
Animals are great! ♪

PETTING ZOO

Elmo is ready for some furry fun, so it's time to visit the petting zoo. The petting zoo is a place where you can pet and feed the animals!

While Elmo feeds a baby chick, search for these animal friends:

this goat

this pig

this horse

this cow

this sheep

this duck

this llama

♪ The pigs at the zoo go oink, oink, oink! Animals are great! ♪

Elmo needs to stand super still at the butterfly exhibit. If he does, a brightly colored butterfly might just land on his nose. That tickles!

Try to keep still while you search for these colorful things at the butterfly exhibit:

this purple butterfly

this red and orange butterfly

this red and orange butterfly

this yellow, orange, and red butterfly

this blue butterfly

this green caterpillar

♪ *The butterflies at the zoo go flutter, flutter, FLAP! Animals are great!* ♪

NO RUNNING AFTER BUTTERFLIES

Elmo's last stop is the coldest…and cutest. Penguins love cold weather, and they have special feathers to keep them warm. Little monsters like Elmo don't have feathers, so they wear jackets!

Try to stay warm while you search around the antarctic exhibit for these penguins:

♪ *The penguins at the zoo go waddle, waddle, SQUAWK! Animals are great!* ♪

There's so much to see and count at the zoo! Go back to the entrance and see if you can find these things:

1 tram

4 zoo workers

2 lions

5 pigeons

3 tigers

6 strollers

Swim back to the sea lion pool and search for these opposites:

a **dry** sea lion

a **wet** sea lion

a **small** sea lion

a **big** sea lion

a sea lion **on** a rock

a sea lion **off** a rock

a **sleeping** sea lion

an **awake** sea lion

a **young** guest

an **old** guest

a **tall** trainer

a **short** trainer

Lots of babies are born at the zoo! Gallop back to the savanna to find these baby animals:

a baby giraffe (calf)

a baby meerkat (pup)

a baby gazelle (fawn)

a baby ostrich (whelp)

a baby elephant (calf)

a baby zebra (foal)

Reptiles and amphibians come in all shapes and sizes. Slither back to the reptile house and find these animals:

a small chameleon

a big, spikey lizard

a thin, long snake

the smallest frog

the biggest frog

Swing back to the monkey house and search for these shapes:

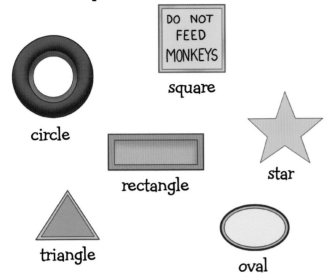

square

circle

rectangle

star

triangle

oval

Animals at the zoo make lots of different sounds. Go back to the petting zoo and look for noisy friends that say:

baaah

quack

peep-peep

mooooo

oink

neigh

Butterflies are so colorful, but they aren't the only colorful things at the zoo. Flutter back to the butterfly house and look for these brightly colored things:

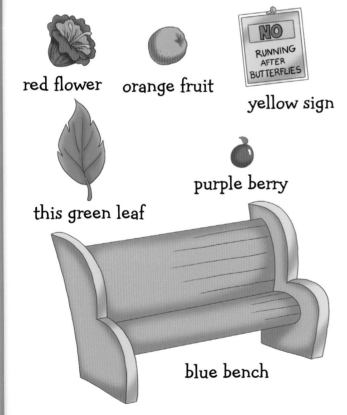

red flower

orange fruit

yellow sign

this green leaf

purple berry

blue bench

Did you miss the penguins? They missed you! Go back to the penguin exhibit and look for these penguins: